MEMORIES FOR MY GRANDCHILD

By ANNIE DECKER and
NICOLE STEPHENSON

Photographs by
JULIE TOY

CHRONICLE BOOKS
680 SECOND STREET
SAN FRANCISCO, CA 94107
WWW.CHRONICLEBOOKS.COM

Text © 2004 Annie Decker and Nicole Stephenson

Photographs © 2004 Julie Toy

ISBN 978-0-8118-4327-0

Design by Kristen M. Nobles

Manufactured in China

10 9 8

Chronicle Books LLC

680 Second Street

San Francisco, CA 94107

www.chroniclebooks.com

Quotation credits:

Ellen Goodman, with permission of The Washington Post Writers Group.

From *Grandmothers Are Like Snowflakes . . . No Two Are Alike* by Janet Lanese, © 1996.

Used by permission of Dell Publishing, a division of Random House, Inc.

From *The Power and the Glory,* Graham Greene, copyright 1940, renewed © 1968 by Graham Greene.

Used by permission of Viking Penguin, a division of Penguin Group (USA) Inc.

Albert Einstein, *Ladies' Home Journal,* December 1946.

Permission of the Albert Einstein Archives, Jewish National and University Library, Jerusalem.

MEMORIES FOR MY GRANDCHILD

TABLE OF CONTENTS

*"What the next generation
will value most is not what we owned,
but the evidence of who we were
and the tales of how we loved."*

—ELLEN GOODMAN

INTRODUCTION

As a grandparent, you get to share your wisdom and teach the youngest members of your family about their connections to their roots and to the world. *Memories for My Grandchild* takes you on the journey of sharing your life. In this book, you will record the broad story as well as the finer details, creating a rich picture of yourself and your family and providing a keepsake everyone will cherish.

By telling your stories, you are helping your grandchild grow closer to the people, places, and times that have shaped and given meaning to you and your family. Each chapter of this book guides you through a different stage of your life, drawing out memories of family and friends, sights and sounds, songs you loved, places you traveled—the experiences of a lifetime and the ones you're still looking forward to.

Memories for My Grandchild also gives you a way to collect photographs, clippings, and other keepsakes to pass on to your grandchild. Any sweet, funny, or classic pictures you place in the photo slots that open each chapter will give life to your words. The envelope at the back of the book can store other treasures—such as letters, recipes, news clippings, ticket stubs, drawings, and still more photographs. Include mementos from your youth, such as report cards, tickets from favorite movies, notes from friends, and pictures from school dances. Add photographs from important events, such as your wedding, holidays, and family vacations. Through these keepsakes, your grandchild will be able to imagine the people and events of your life.

The simplest way to start is just to grab a pen and begin, but here are a few tips to help you along the way:

• To get your memories flowing, look through some of the photographs, papers, and other mementos you've saved through the years, and talk with your friends and loved ones about important times in your life.

• Move at your own pace, as quickly or as slowly as feels right. Answer the questions in any order, and feel free to skip some or add your own.

• Fill out the book with your grandchild and see how much more you learn about yourself—and your grandchild—as you go. Consider letting your family interview you on audiotape or on video.

• You, your family, and your experiences are all unique, so adapt the questions as you wish. This book is about *you*.

• The dedication page provides space for one grandchild, but you can adapt it for more grandchildren if you like.

Most important, have fun! There's never as good a time as today to begin.

"Grandchildren are loving reminders
of what we're really here for."
—JANET LANESE

FOR MY GRANDCHILD

This book is dedicated to: ....
(grandchild's name)

Dear .... ,
(grandchild's name)

I have created this book of memories for you because: ....
....
....

The first time I saw you: ....
....
....

You were: .... old.

We were in the city/town of: ....

You looked like: ....
....

I felt: ....
....

When I tell my friends about you, I say: ....
....

As you go through life, always remember: ....
....

Love always,

....
(your name)

....
(today's date)

Roots

*"To forget one's ancestors is to be a brook without a source,
a tree without a root."*

—Chinese proverb

....
(grandchild)   (grandchild)   (grandchild)

....
(child)   (spouse)

....
....
(siblings)   (siblings)

....
....
(my parents)

....
....
(my grandparents)

OUR FAMILY TREE

Include the names and birthdates of your family members.
Adapt the tree as you wish to include more ancestors
or to accommodate different family structures.

OUR ANCESTORS

What are your roots? How far back does your knowledge of your family history go? The next few questions are about your great-grandparents and other ancestors whose stories have been passed down.

Where did your ancestors live? If they moved from a different country, do you know when, why, and how?

....

....

....

....

....

....

....

....

What do you know about the towns, cities, or countries in which they lived? What languages did they speak?

....

....

....

....

....

....

....

....

OUR ANCESTORS

Tell any interesting or unusual stories about your ancestors.

....

....

....

....

....

....

What do you know about the origins and meanings of your family's last names? Have any of these names been changed over time? Why?

....

....

....

....

....

Do you feel a special connection with any of your ancestors? With whom, and why?

....

....

....

....

....

OUR ANCESTORS

Have you visited any of the places your family originally came from, or met relatives who still live there? What did you gain from the experience?

....

....

....

....

....

....

....

....

....

Has your family had any famous or infamous members? What did they do?

....

....

....

....

....

....

....

....

....

....

MY GRANDPARENTS

What names did you use for your grandparents?

....

....

What stories have you heard about your grandparents when they were young?

....

....

....

....

....

....

How did they meet? What have you heard about their courtship?

....

....

....

....

....

What did they do for a living? Did they have any hobbies or other activities?

....

....

....

....

....

....

MY GRANDPARENTS

Did they speak any other languages?

....

....

What were some of their favorite sayings or expressions?

....

....

....

Did your grandparents live near you when you were growing up? If not, where did they live?

How often did you see them?

....

....

....

....

Did you ever stay with your grandparents? Were there any special activities you used to

do together?

....

....

....

....

....

....

MY GRANDPARENTS

What is your fondest memory of your grandparents?

....

....

....

....

....

What did you learn about life from your grandparents?

....

....

....

....

....

How old were you when they passed away?

....

....

....

....

....

MY PARENTS

Are your parents still living? If they passed away, what were the circumstances?

What names do/did you use for your parents?

What names do/did they use for each other?

Do/did your parents speak any other languages?

What are/were some of their favorite expressions?

MY PARENTS: GROWING UP

Where did your parents grow up? Did they move around a lot while growing up?

....

....

....

....

....

....

....

Do/did they have brothers and sisters? Older or younger? Do/did they tell any memorable

stories about playing together?

....

....

....

....

....

....

....

MY PARENTS: GROWING UP

Where did your parents go to school, from grade school to high school or beyond? Did they enjoy any activities or sports when they were younger?

....

....

....

....

....

....

....

....

Do you have any favorite stories about your parents when they were young?

....

....

....

....

....

....

....

....

....

MY PARENTS: AS ADULTS

Did your parents move away from home when they grew up? Why, or why not?

....

....

....

....

....

....

....

....

Tell the story of how your parents met. What do you know about their courtship?

....

....

....

....

....

....

....

....

MY PARENTS: AS ADULTS

What do you know about your parents' wedding day? Did they go on a honeymoon? If so, where?

....

....

....

....

....

....

....

....

What do/did your parents do for a living? How many hours a week do they work? Did one of them stay at home while you where young?

....

....

....

....

....

....

....

....

....

MY PARENTS: AS ADULTS

How do/did your parents get around? Bicycle? Bus? Train? Car? Foot?

What do/did they like to do with their free time?

MY PARENTS: AS ADULTS

What sort of music do/did your parents like? Do/did they like to sing or dance?

....

....

....

....

....

....

....

....

Did your parents have different ideas about parenting? What were each of their strengths and responsibilities as parents?

....

....

....

....

....

....

....

....

....

MY PARENTS: AS ADULTS

Did your family ever struggle to make ends meet? Has that experience influenced the way you've chosen to live your life?

In what ways today do you look or act like your parents?

What lessons about life have you learned from your parents?

MY EXTENDED FAMILY

List the names of the relatives who make up your extended family, with a note about how each of them is related to you.

....

....

....

....

....

....

....

....

....

Write down what you remember about your great-aunts and great-uncles, aunts and uncles, cousins, or others in your extended family.

....

....

....

....

....

....

....

....

....

....

....

....

MY EXTENDED FAMILY

Did you see any of them often while you were growing up? What did you do together?

....

....

....

....

....

....

....

Who else has been "part of the family" even though they were not related by blood or marriage?

....

....

....

....

....

Did you have favorite relatives or family friends you looked up to? Who were they, and why were they important to you?

....

....

....

....

....

....

MY EXTENDED FAMILY

Did you gather with extended family for holidays or other celebrations? Which ones?

....

....

....

....

....

....

....

....

Are you still close with any of your extended family members? If so, who?

....

....

....

....

....

....

....

....

....

....

MY EXTENDED FAMILY

Have you been to any family reunions? Describe when, where, who came, and what you did together.

....

....

....

....

....

Do any traits or interests run in the family?

....

....

....

....

....

Does your family have a special burial place? Where?

....

....

....

....

....

SNAPSHOT OF A SPECIAL TIME

Think of a time when you and your family shared a cherished moment—maybe it was around the holidays, during the summer, or while on vacation, or perhaps your family had a special evening once a week. Share the place, time, season, and sensations you remember:

....

....

....

....

What made this time meaningful to you?

....

....

....

....

....

Sketch part or all of the scene...

"There is always one moment in childhood
when the door opens and lets the future in."

GRAHAM GREENE

AS A CHILD

My address was:

The view from my bedroom window was:

In the morning, I woke up at about:

At night, I went to sleep at about:

My hairstyle was:

I loved to wear:

A favorite food was:

My best friend was:

My nicknames were:

I spent most of my free time:

I got around by (bicycle, bus, train, car, foot):

My pets were:

My most prized possession was:

A gift I loved receiving was:

I earned $ an hour doing:

My favorite book was:

My favorite movie was:

My favorite radio or television show was:

My favorite music, singer, or band was:

My favorite hobby was:

My favorite sport was:

My hero was:

My dream was to:

My biggest concern was:

My greatest accomplishment was:

A significant world event was:

HOME LIFE

I was born at _____ on _____ in _____
                  (time)   (date)   (city/town, state/region, and country)

Were you born in a hospital, at home, or somewhere else?

....

....

....

....

Do you know any stories about the time leading up to your birth?

....

....

....

....

....

How did your parents choose your name?

....

....

....

....

....

HOME LIFE

What are your earliest memories?

....

....

....

....

....

....

Describe your childhood home, pretending you are walking in the front door and giving someone a tour.

....

....

....

....

....

....

What did your bedroom look like? Did you share it with anyone?

....

....

....

....

....

HOME LIFE

Did you have a favorite stuffed animal, blanket, or toy?

What is a special moment you shared with your mother when you were a child?
With your father?

Do you have brothers and sisters? Older or younger? How close or far apart are you in age?

HOME LIFE

What are some things you did with your siblings—games you played or experiences you shared?

....

....

....

....

....

....

....

Did you ever fight with your siblings? If so, what did you fight about?

....

....

....

....

....

....

Were you especially close with any of your siblings?

....

....

....

....

....

HOME LIFE

Did any relatives live with you and your family? For how long?

Did any relatives or baby-sitters regularly take care of you? Anybody you especially liked or disliked?

Did you have any chores? What were they and how did you feel about having to do them?

HOME LIFE

What were some of the rules you had to follow when you were a child?

Did you think they were fair?

What world events do you remember your parents talking about? What were their political views?

HOME LIFE

Did your parents raise you according to a specific religion or other spiritual teaching?
If so, how was it a part of your life? Was it similar to how they were raised?

How did your family spend evenings together?

What were family meals like? What dishes did you often eat?

BIRTHDAYS, VACATIONS, AND SPECIAL EVENTS

Do you have a favorite childhood birthday memory?

Did your parents take you out to any special events (plays, concerts, festivals, sporting events, etc.)? Which ones did you enjoy most?

BIRTHDAYS, VACATIONS, AND SPECIAL EVENTS

Did you take family vacations? Where to? Which one(s) did you like best?

Which were your favorite holidays? Why?

BIRTHDAYS, VACATIONS, AND SPECIAL EVENTS

Describe the flavors and aromas of the food served at your home during the holidays. Do you make any of those dishes yourself now?

Include a recipe for a favorite holiday dish or meal here.

MY HOMETOWN

Describe your hometown. What did you like and dislike about growing up there?

Describe your neighborhood and neighbors. What made your neighborhood unique?

Sketch a map of your childhood neighborhood, including your home and the places that were important to you, such as parks, favorite stores, schools, and friends' houses.

MY HOMETOWN

Did your family move during your childhood years? Where? How did you feel about moving?

In what ways has your hometown changed since you were a child?

SCHOOL AND FRIENDS

Where did you go to

Preschool:
....
(name of school)   (location)   (years attended)

Kindergarten:
....
(name of school)   (location)   (years attended)

Elementary school:
....
(name of school)   (location)   (years attended)

Junior high school:
....
(name of school)   (location)   (years attended)

How far did you have to travel to school? How did you get there?

Which subjects did you like best, and which did you like least?

Did you sing, act, or play any musical instruments?

Is there a teacher you remember fondly? One you didn't like?

What games did you play at recess?

SCHOOL AND FRIENDS

Who were your closest friends?

What did you do when you played together?

Did you have a secret hiding place?

Did you and your friends ever get into trouble? What for?

Did you have a childhood sweetheart?

What did you say you wanted to be when you grew up?

IN RETROSPECT

Which of these words best describe you as a child?

☐ Playful   ☐ Thoughtful   ☐ Shy   ☐ Mischievous

☐ Outgoing   ☐ Imaginative   ☐ Sporty   ☐ _____

What about you has stayed the same since childhood?

....

....

....

....

....

....

....

....

What happened during your childhood that strongly influenced the adult you grew up to be?

....

....

....

....

....

....

....

SNAPSHOT OF A SPECIAL TIME

Think of a vivid childhood memory you hold dear, and describe the place, time, season, and sensations you remember:

What made this time meaningful to you?

Sketch part or all of the scene...

TEENAGE YEARS

"Light tomorrow with today!"

—Elizabeth Barrett Browning

AS A TEENAGER

My address was:

The view from my bedroom window was:

In the morning, I woke up at about:

At night, I went to sleep at about:

My hairstyle was:

I loved to wear:

A favorite food was:

My best friend was:

My nicknames were:

I spent most of my free time:

I often spent Saturday nights:

I got around by (bicycle, bus, train, car, foot):

My pets were:

My most prized possession was:

A gift I loved receiving was:

I earned $ an hour doing:

My favorite book was:

My favorite movie was:

My favorite radio or television show was:

My favorite music, singer, or band was:

My favorite hobby was:

My hero was:

My dream was to:

My biggest concern was:

My greatest accomplishment was:

A significant world event was:

HOME LIFE

What did your bedroom look like? Did you share it with anyone?

....

....

....

....

....

....

....

....

If you had siblings, what did you do together?

....

....

....

....

....

....

....

How did you get along with your siblings? What did you fight about? When did you have the most fun together?

....

....

....

....

....

....

....

HOME LIFE

What did your family do in the evenings? What were common topics of conversation?

....

....

....

....

....

....

....

When did you spend time with your parents? What did you most like doing together?

....

....

....

....

....

....

Did you want to follow in either of your parents' footsteps?

....

....

....

....

....

....

....

HOME LIFE

Do you remember a good heart-to-heart you had with one of your parents? What did you talk about?

....

....

....

....

....

Is there anything you wish you had talked about with your parents?

....

....

....

....

....

....

What rules did you have to follow about curfews, going to friends' houses, dating, and so on? Did you think they were fair? Did you ever try to get around them?

....

....

....

....

....

HOME LIFE

What did you think about religion and spirituality as a teenager?

What did you do during summer vacations?

What is the farthest you had been from home without your family by the time you left high school?

SCHOOL AND FRIENDS

Which subjects or teachers inspired you? With which subjects or teachers did you have a hard time?

Is there a paper or project you enjoyed working on?

Do you remember any embarrassing high school moments?

SCHOOL AND FRIENDS

Did you play sports or participate in other school activities?

....

....

....

....

....

....

Did you receive any awards for your studies, sports, or other activities?

....

....

....

....

....

....

Did you have a job or volunteer for any community organizations? What did you do?

....

....

....

....

....

....

SCHOOL AND FRIENDS

Who were your closest friends?

....

....

....

....

What did you do together? Did you have any favorite hangouts?

....

....

....

....

....

What did you like to talk about?

....

....

....

....

....

What did you and your friends do that now seems risky or foolish? Would you do it again?

....

....

....

....

SCHOOL AND FRIENDS

Did you have a crush on anyone? Did he or she know it?

....

....

....

....

....

....

Did you have a boyfriend or girlfriend? How long did you date?

....

....

....

....

....

....

What do you remember about your prom or other social events?

....

....

....

....

....

....

SCHOOL AND FRIENDS

What were the biggest fashion trends? What did you wear to parties or to dances?

....

....

....

....

....

What kind of music did you listen to? What did your parents think of it?

....

....

....

....

....

Were you a fan of any movie stars, musicians, sports figures, or other celebrities?

....

....

....

....

....

FIRST EXPERIENCES

Tell the stories of your "firsts"—how old you were, the people you were with, and your thoughts at the time.

Your first school dance:

....

....

....

....

Your first date:

....

....

....

....

Your first kiss:

....

....

....

....

The first lesson you learned about love:

....

....

....

....

FIRST EXPERIENCES

The first time you drove a car:

....

....

....

....

Your first broken bone or scar:

....

....

....

....

....

The first time you tried drinking or smoking:

....

....

....

....

Another "first" you remember well:

....

....

....

....

....

GROWING UP

Rank the following in order of importance to you as a teenager, from 1 (most important) to 9 (least important):

☐ School	☐ Friends	☐ Family	☐ Sports
☐ Religion/spirituality	☐ Jobs	☐ Dating	☐ Hobbies
☐ Other:			

What did you want to do when you got older, as a career or otherwise? What clues in your life as a teenager pointed to what you later ended up doing?

....

....

....

....

....

....

....

....

....

....

....

....

....

....

GROWING UP

If you could go back and be a teenager again, what is one thing you would do differently?

It would be better to be a teenager in today's world because:

It was better to be a teenager back then because:

SNAPSHOT OF A SPECIAL TIME

Think of a memory that captures what it was like to be a teenager, and describe the place, time, season, and sensations you remember:

What made this time meaningful to you?

Sketch part or all of the scene...

ENTERING ADULTHOOD

"Hitch your wagon to a star."

—RALPH WALDO EMERSON

AS A YOUNG ADULT

My address was:

The view from my bedroom window was:

In the morning, I woke up at about:

At night, I went to sleep at about:

My hairstyle was:

I loved to wear:

A favorite food was:

My best friend was:

My nicknames were:

I spent most of my free time:

I often spent Saturday nights:

I got around by (bicycle, bus, train, car, foot):

My pets were:

My most prized possession was:

A gift I loved receiving was:

I earned $ an hour doing:

My favorite book was:

My favorite movie was:

My favorite radio or television show was:

My favorite music, singer, or band was:

My favorite sport was:

My hero was:

My dream was to:

My biggest concern was:

My greatest accomplishment was:

A significant world event was:

OUT IN THE WORLD

Describe the first time you lived apart from your family. In what ways were you glad to be on your own? What did you miss about home?

....

....

....

....

....

....

Did you stay in touch with your childhood and teenage friends as you got older? How did the relationships evolve over the years?

....

....

....

....

....

Where did you live? Did you move to a different city or town? Did you live in a dorm, an apartment, or a house?

....

....

....

....

....

OUT IN THE WORLD

Did you live with other people? Do you have any funny stories about living with roommates?
Did you ever live by yourself?

....

....

....

....

....

....

....

Did you more often cook for yourself or go out to eat?

....

....

....

....

....

....

What goals did you have as you started out on your own? How did they compare to your
parents' ideas for you?

....

....

....

....

....

....

OUT IN THE WORLD

When did you first think of yourself as an adult?

How did your relationship with your parents change as you became an adult?

What are some lessons you learned about life, or about how the world works, once you were living on your own?

OUT IN THE WORLD

What new people did you meet, or what new ideas did you encounter, that changed the way you looked at the world?

....

....

....

....

....

....

....

....

....

....

Who were your closest friends during your twenties? What kinds of things did you like to do together?

....

....

....

....

....

....

....

....

....

....

....

....

....

....

OUT IN THE WORLD

Did you have any important romantic relationships at this time of your life? How long did
they last? What did you learn from them?

....

....

....

....

....

....

If you didn't marry during this time, did you have a long relationship with anyone?

....

....

....

....

....

....

....

....

What new experiences did you discover as you began to make your way in the world?

....

....

....

....

....

....

OUT IN THE WORLD

Did you go to any political rallies or protests?

Did you join any groups? Volunteer?

OUT IN THE WORLD

Did you travel? Where, and with whom? How did the experience shape your perspective?

If you joined the military, when and where did you go, and what were your duties? How did serving in the military affect your life?

FURTHER EDUCATION

If you went to college or vocational school, or had any other further schooling, where did you go? Why did you choose to go there?

....

....

....

What did you study, and why? Did you earn any degrees?

....

....

....

....

....

What classes, teachers, or projects made an impression on you? How did they influence your future path?

....

....

....

....

Did you join any clubs, teams, or other student organizations?

....

....

....

....

....

....

....

FURTHER EDUCATION

Who were your close friends during school? What did you have in common?

....

....

....

....

....

....

....

What adventures did you have together?

....

....

....

....

....

Did you hold a job during school? Who was responsible for paying your tuition and living expenses?

....

....

....

....

....

FURTHER EDUCATION

How did you spend your summers during college?

In what ways did you grow between the time you started college and when you finished?

WORK

Describe one of your first part-time or full-time jobs. How did you find it? What did you do? (Feel free to adapt these questions for any volunteer work with which you were involved.)

What do you remember about your first job interviews?

What do you remember about the people you worked for?

WORK

What did you wear to work? Was it different from the clothes you were used to wearing?

What did you do after work? Did you spend time with your coworkers?

How did you balance other aspects of your life with your work?

WORK

In what ways was the working world how you expected it to be? In what ways were you surprised by it?

....

....

....

....

....

How long did you stay at your various jobs? Did they build on one another, or did you try working in different fields?

....

....

....

....

....

What strengths did you discover you had?

....

....

....

....

....

SNAPSHOT OF A SPECIAL TIME

Think of a vivid memory from your early adulthood, and describe the place, time, season, and sensations you remember:

....

....

....

....

....

....

What made this time meaningful to you?

....

....

....

....

....

....

Sketch part or all of the scene...

FAMILY LIFE

"Come live with me and be my love . . ."

—JOHN DONNE

WHEN I STARTED A FAMILY

My address was:

The view from my bedroom window was:

In the morning, I woke up at about:

At night, I went to sleep at about:

My hairstyle was:

I loved to wear:

A favorite food was:

My best friend was:

My nicknames were:

I spent most of my free time:

I often spent Saturday nights:

I got around by (bicycle, bus, train, car, foot):

Our pets were:

My most prized possession was:

A gift I loved receiving was:

A special treat I liked to buy myself was:

A movie ticket cost:

My favorite book was:

My favorite movie was:

My favorite radio or television show was:

My favorite music, singer, or band was:

My hero was:

My dream was to:

My biggest concern was:

My greatest accomplishment was:

A significant world event was:

TYING THE KNOT

Feel free to adapt this section for remarriages or for other long-term relationships.

How did you meet your husband or wife?

....

....

....

....

What attracted you to each other at first?

....

....

....

....

Do you remember your first date? What did you do? How old were you?

....

....

....

....

What were your favorite things to do together?

....

....

....

....

....

TYING THE KNOT

As you got to know your future spouse, what made you fall in love with him or her? What did you most admire?

....

....

....

....

....

....

How long did you date before you got engaged?

....

....

Describe the marriage proposal. Where were you? Was the proposal a surprise? What did each of you say?

....

....

....

....

....

....

....

....

....

TYING THE KNOT

Tell the story of your wedding day. When and where was your wedding? What kind of ceremony did you have? Did you follow any traditions? Did you do anything unconventional? What roles did friends and family play? Do you remember any toasts your guests made? Do you have a favorite moment from the day?

TYING THE KNOT

Did you go on a honeymoon? If so, where? Describe your memories from the trip.

LIFE TOGETHER

What was your first home together like?

....

....

....

....

....

....

Describe a typical day in the early part of your marriage.

....

....

....

....

....

....

Was there anything about being married that surprised you?

....

....

....

....

....

....

LIFE TOGETHER

Describe one of your best memories from early in your marriage.

What difficulties did you face?

How long have you been married? Describe one or two of your favorite moments as a couple.

LIFE TOGETHER

What advice can you offer on how to have a happy relationship?

....

....

....

....

....

How have you celebrated your anniversaries throughout the years?

....

....

....

....

....

....

If you got divorced, what led to that decision? Have you been in any important romantic relationships since?

....

....

....

....

....

....

BECOMING A PARENT

What was happening in your life before your first child was born?

....

....

....

....

....

How did your life change after the baby?

....

....

....

....

....

....

How many children do you have? How did you choose their names? (If you adopted children,

describe the experience.)

....

....

....

....

....

....

BECOMING A PARENT

Did you and your partner have different ideas about parenting? What were each of your strengths and responsibilities as parents?

....

....

....

....

....

....

....

....

If you had more than one child, how did they get along with each other when they were young?

....

....

....

....

....

....

....

....

....

BECOMING A PARENT:
RAISING MY GRANDCHILD'S PARENT

In the following section, your grandchild will get to learn new things specifically about his or her parent.

What do you remember about the pregnancy with this son or daughter?

....

....

....

....

Tell the story of this child's birth.

....

....

....

....

Do you remember his or her first words?

....

....

....

Do you remember when he or she first walked?

....

....

....

Any other memorable "firsts"?

....

....

....

BECOMING A PARENT:
RAISING MY GRANDCHILD'S PARENT

What was your son or daughter's favorite...

Lullaby:

Bedtime story:

Toy, stuffed animal, or doll:

Game:

Birthday party:

Halloween costume:

Place to play:

Describe your son or daughter's personality and how it changed through the years. Did he or she remind you of any other family members?

BECOMING A PARENT:
RAISING MY GRANDCHILD'S PARENT

Describe a special moment you shared with your son or daughter in his or her childhood.

....

....

....

....

....

What is something your child did as a teenager that made you realize he or she was growing up?

....

....

....

....

....

Describe first learning your son or daughter was going to become a parent. Where were you? How did you feel?

....

....

....

....

BECOMING A PARENT:
RAISING MY CHILDREN

Was there anything your parents did when they were raising you that you wanted to repeat with your own children? Anything you did not want to repeat?

....

....

....

....

....

....

Did your parents help you raise your children? Did anyone else lend a hand?

....

....

....

....

....

Did you raise your children with any specific religious or spiritual beliefs?

....

....

....

....

....

....

....

....

....

BECOMING A PARENT:
RAISING MY CHILDREN

Tell a story about taking one of your children to school for the first time, or another school experience.

How did you celebrate holidays and birthdays?

What rules did you expect your children to follow? Did they think your rules were fair? Did they try to get around any of them?

BECOMING A PARENT:
RAISING MY CHILDREN

In what ways were you involved in your children's school or extracurricular activities?

....

....

....

....

....

....

How did your relationship with your children change as they got older?

....

....

....

....

....

....

At what moments did you feel especially proud of them?

....

....

....

....

....

....

BECOMING A PARENT:
LOOKING BACK

What do you admire about the choices your children have made as adults?

....

....

....

....

....

....

....

....

....

What are some of your children's most special achievements?

....

....

....

....

....

....

....

....

....

....

....

....

BECOMING A PARENT:
LOOKING BACK

Are there any experiences your children have had that you would have liked to experience yourself?

....

....

....

....

....

....

....

Have you experienced anything you wish they could have experienced as well?

....

....

....

....

....

....

....

BECOMING A PARENT:
LOOKING BACK

What is the most rewarding thing about being a parent?

....

....

....

....

....

....

....

What is the hardest part about being a parent?

....

....

....

....

....

....

....

What have you learned from being a parent?

....

....

....

....

....

....

FRIENDS AND FAMILY

With which of your friends from earlier days did you remain close as you raised your children? Did you see them often?

....

....

....

....

....

....

What new friends came into your life? How did you meet them?

....

....

....

....

....

....

What is your relationship like with your siblings as adults? How is it different from when you were younger?

....

....

....

....

....

SNAPSHOT OF A SPECIAL TIME

Think of a fond memory from when your grandchild's mother or father was growing up, and describe the place, time, season, and sensations you remember:

....

....

....

....

....

What made this time meaningful to you?

....

....

....

....

....

....

Sketch part or all of the scene...

TODAY

"Life can only be understood backwards,
but it must be lived forwards."

—SØREN KIERKEGAARD

TODAY

My address is:

The view from my bedroom window is:

In the morning, I wake up at about:

At night, I go to sleep at about:

My hairstyle is:

I love to wear:

My favorite food is:

My best friend is:

My nicknames are:

I spend my free time:

My favorite activity with my grandchild is:

I get around by (bicycle, bus, train, car, foot):

My pets are:

My most prized possession is:

A gift I loved receiving recently is:

A movie ticket costs:

The best book I read recently is:

The best movie I saw recently is:

My favorite radio or television show is:

My favorite music, singer, or band is:

A sport I enjoy is:

A person I greatly admire is:

My dream is to:

My biggest concern is:

A satisfying recent accomplishment was:

A recent significant world event was:

A TIMELINE OF MY LIFE

Fill in the timeline below with the events that have been most important to you. You can include family, personal, community, and world events—whatever you consider to be the milestones in your life.

Date	Event

"Life is not dated merely by years. Events are sometimes the best calendars."

—BENJAMIN DISRAELI

HOME LIFE

Where have you lived as an adult? List the places and the years you lived there. Which were your favorites? Why?

....

....

....

....

Do any family members live with you?

....

....

....

....

What is your favorite meal to cook? Do you have a specialty? If so, share the recipe here:

....

....

....

....

....

....

....

....

....

HOME LIFE

Do you follow any routines? Do you do anything now that you didn't do earlier in your life?

Do you have a favorite time of day, or a favorite season, when you love to be at home?

What do you do to relax?

Are you working on any projects at home or in your community?

HOME LIFE

If you are married or in a relationship with someone special...

What does he or she do for work? (If retired, what was his or her job?)

....
....

What do you enjoy doing together?

....
....

What do you disagree about?

....
....

What do you love most about him or her?

....
....

What else do you want your grandchildren to know about him or her?

....
....
....
....

What moments in your life together have been especially important to you?

....
....
....
....
....

FRIENDS

Who are your closest friends? Do you live near each other?

....

....

....

Which friends, or groups of friends, do you get together with regularly? What do you do together? What do you value in those friendships?

....

....

....

....

....

....

Which friendships have lasted through thick and thin?

....

....

....

Which faraway friends and loved ones do you most often call, write, or e-mail?

....

....

....

....

WORK AND COMMUNITY

Have you found your calling in a certain field, either as a paid worker or a volunteer? How did you find your way to it?

....
....
....
....
....
....

How have your goals evolved through the years?

....
....
....
....
....
....
....

What are some of your most satisfying accomplishments at work or in the community?

....
....
....
....
....
....
....

WORK AND COMMUNITY

When do you plan to retire? What are some things you want to do when you retire?

If you've already retired, what was it like to stop working? How is your life different now?

Is there another line of work that always intrigued you, a dream job you wish you'd had or you plan to have?

REFLECTIONS

How would you describe yourself and your outlook on life now?

What do you think your friends and loved ones value most about you?

What do you value most about yourself?

REFLECTIONS

How have your religious or spiritual beliefs evolved over the years?

....

....

....

....

....

....

How has your health been throughout your life?

....

....

....

....

....

....

....

....

What has surprised you about growing older?

....

....

....

....

....

....

....

REFLECTIONS

What sayings or quotations do you often repeat?

What is the most adventurous thing you've done in the past ten years?

If you could travel anywhere in the world, where would you go? With whom?

REFLECTIONS

What do you think matters most in life?

Is there a piece of wisdom that has helped you through life? Where or whom does it come from?

What are you most proud of in your life?

REFLECTIONS:
BEING A GRANDPARENT

How did you feel when you first learned you were going to be a grandparent?

....

....

....

....

How many grandchildren do you have? What are their names and ages?

....

....

....

....

What do you like to do with them?

....

....

....

....

What family tradition would you like to see your grandchildren carry on?

....

....

....

....

....

REFLECTIONS:
BEING A GRANDPARENT

Have you saved anything to pass on to your grandchildren?

What place would you love your grandchildren to visit? Why?

What are your hopes for your grandchildren?

What's one thing your grandchild might not know about you that you would like to share?

"Grandchildren and grandparents are joined at the heart."

—SOURCE UNKNOWN

LOOKING BACK
AND LOOKING AHEAD

Describe a defining moment or turning point in your life. What happened? How did your life change? Do you think it changed for the better?

....

....

....

....

....

What have been the most astonishing inventions of your lifetime? What did you think about them when they first appeared? What do you think of them now?

....

....

....

....

....

Where were you at the time of two or three major historical events, and what effects did they have on you and your world?

....

....

....

....

....

LOOKING BACK
AND LOOKING AHEAD

Do you still hold the same political views as you did earlier in life?

Who is your favorite public figure of all time? Why?

Is there a phrase you can think of that describes your generation well?

LOOKING BACK
AND LOOKING AHEAD

What have been your generation's greatest challenges and achievements?

What changes in the world have you observed, and what changes do you expect in the future?

Which president did you admire the most? Why?

LOOKING BACK
AND LOOKING AHEAD

What class would you like to take, or what skill would you like to learn?

What travel or other experiences are you looking forward to?

What special events are you looking forward to celebrating?

SNAPSHOT OF A SPECIAL TIME

Think of a vivid memory with your grandchild, something or someplace you hold dear, and describe the place, time, season, and sensations you remember:

....

....

....

....

....

What made this time meaningful to you?

....

....

....

....

....

....

Sketch part or all of the scene...

FURTHER THOUGHTS

Use this space to write down any other comments you would like to make, pictures you would like to draw, or stories you need more room to tell.

FURTHER THOUGHTS

FURTHER THOUGHTS

RESOURCES

Your own family is a wonderful resource you can draw on to learn about your personal history as well as that of your more distant ancestors. Below are other resources that will help you collect the stories of your family throughout the generations.

BOOKS

Carmack, Sharon DeBartolo. *A Genealogist's Guide to Discovering Your Immigrant and Ethnic Ancestors: How to Find and Record Your Unique Heritage.* Cincinnati, Ohio: Betterway Books, 2000.

Croom, Emily Anne. *Unpuzzling Your Past: The Best-Selling Basic Guide to Genealogy,* 4th ed. Cincinnati, Ohio: Betterway Books, 2003.

Epstein, Ellen, and Jane Lewit. *Record and Remember: Tracing Your Roots Through Oral History.* Lanham, Md.: Scarborough House, 1994.

Everton Publishers, et al. *The Handybook for Genealogists: United States of America,* 10th ed. Cincinnati, Ohio: F&W Publications, 2002.

Fletcher, William. *Recording Your Family History: A Guide to Preserving Oral History, Videotape, Audiotape, Suggested Topics and Questions, Interview Techniques.* Berkeley, Calif.: Ten Speed Press, 1989.

Hendrickson, Nancy. *Finding Your Roots Online.* Cincinnati, Ohio: Betterway Books, 2003.

Renick, Barbara. *Genealogy 101: How to Trace Your Family's History and Heritage.* Nashville, Tenn.: Rutledge Hill Press, 2003.

Ritchie, Donald A. *Doing Oral History: A Practical Guide,* 2nd ed. New York: Oxford University Press, 2003.

Rosenbluth, Vera. *Keeping Family Stories Alive: Discovering and Recording the Stories and Reflections of a Lifetime,* rev. ed. Berkeley, Calif.: Hartley & Marks, 1997.

Spence, Linda. *Legacy: A Step-By-Step Guide to Writing Personal History.* Athens, Ohio: Ohio University Press, 1997.

Taylor, Maureen A. *Uncovering Your Ancestry Through Family Photographs.* Cincinnati, Ohio: Betterway Books, 2000.

RESOURCES

LIBRARIES, HISTORICAL SOCIETIES, AND OTHER LOCAL RESOURCES

Your local public institutions, and the staff in particular, are excellent genealogical resources. Both before and after identifying the ancestors whose lives you are researching, you can visit your local libraries, archives, historical societies, and museums and find out what information they can share with you and what other tips they might have.

INTERNET RESOURCES

Many resources are available on the Internet. Through simple searches, you can find a great deal of useful information about preserving recorded interviews and researching family history. Helpful words to search for include "ancestry," "oral history," "genealogy," and "autobiography." You also can find databases of personal historians who can help you put together a family history. The following list of Web sites will guide you down these paths:

- Ideas Factory: www.ideasfactory.com/bigidea/howto/build.shtml
  A site with instructions about how to put audiotape and video interviews onto the Internet.

- Ancestry.com: www.ancestry.com
  One of the main host sites for a range of family-tree and ancestry research topics.

- Cyndi's List of Genealogy Sites on the Internet: www.cyndislist.com
  Provides a comprehensive survey of genealogy Web sites and offers many categorized links.

- The Genealogy Home Page: www.genhomepage.com
  Organized by topic; keeps track of hundreds of genealogy links and updates its list daily.

- FamilySearch Internet Genealogy Service: www.familysearch.org
  Provided by the Church of Jesus Christ of Latter-Day Saints, renowned for its genealogical resources. You can search the Ancestral File, the International Genealogical Index, the Pedigree Resource File, and a list of various Web sites.

- About.com: Genealogy: www.genealogy.about.com
  Organizes links to Web sites on various topics and provides how-to links such as Genealogy 101, Writing Your Family's History, and Research & Records, leading you to sources such as military records. Feature articles on various topics also appear regularly.

- A Barrel of Genealogy Links: www.cpcug.org/user/jlacombe/mark.html
  Offers access to hundreds of Internet resources.